# Exploring the Roots of Human Emotion
## In Sculpture

A description of the evolution of the formative processes
of the Human Emotions that are common to all people
in the sculpture of

## Nathan Cabot Hale, PhD, ANA, FNSS

Photographs by
Jerry L. Thompson for
The White Whale Press
and
The Ages of Man Foundation
New York

ISBN 978-0-9640029-2-0

Library of Congress Catalog Card Number 2007930441

Published by White Whale Press
Amenia, New York

Printed and bound in the United States of America

# Contents
# (sculpture and commentary)

# ACKNOWLEDGMENTS

Alison Hale

Dr. Lisa Hale Rose

Amy Lynne Brown, MA

Dr. Niels Berg

Dr. Arthur Nelson

Dr. Martin Salwen

Dr. Robin R. Karpf

Dr. Gary F. Karpf

# DEDICATION

For
Brigitte

Who has led me
To
The River of Life

And To
Olivia

# FOREWORD

No one
Owns
The Truth

For Truth is a State
Of Being
In the
Body
As it Swims
In the Sea of Energy
That
Surrounds
The Planet
And
The Universe

We can only
Live Within
The Truth

# My Studies of the Human Figure

To begin this discussion of my work with the human figure in sculpture I must say that it has actually been a personal exploration of my soul as it emerges from the energy processes of nature and all life. I believe that we all are a part of the energy processes of the planet and that we have slowly evolved from the earth, sea and sky. I also believe that mankind represents, as Jesus said, *The Temple of God.*

I was named Nathan Cabot Hale for my father, my grandfather and my grandfather's uncle . . . all of them were named Nathan . . . it was a family tradition. My name has often been something of a problem to others because of its historic connotations and the assumptions they made about it. To me it was simply a nice sounding label for the person inside my body. Yet I learned at an early age that it was not an ordinary name, and that it bore a heavy weight of implication that had nothing whatever to do with the small boy who has carried it since his beginning. However, this name put a certain responsibility on me that I have felt obliged to come to terms with. I eventually was able to understand my name inferred a certain responsibility and I gradually was able to see a greater meaning in it. My name has enabled me to gain an historical perspective on life.

Let us clear up this matter of names: Names are merely labels for our human organisms . . . and human organisms have far greater significance than their labels. Once I had understood this fact about people's names, I was able to look for the real personages beneath their *given* social labels. I began to see that the stance, the hair and eye color and the general attitude were more important factors than the names. I began to marvel at the immense variety of human meaning that was always hidden beneath the outer label. And I soon learned to respond to people with a deeper perception. Because of this, I did not always fit into the polite society of groups and schools. Yet life was always a great adventure for me, for I soon began to see beyond the side-shows, shams and pretensions of the world. I became something of a character analyst . . . and oddly, because of this, I later was attracted to the theater and acting. And I actually became an actor for a while . . . until I decided that the "World *was not* a Stage.

As a boy I was encouraged in my analytic and scientific traits by my mother who, when I was seven, explained to me the origin of life and the birth process. She showed me these processes in the Gray's Anatomy she was studying in her nurses training. Let me tell you that I was astounded at seeing the origin and growth of the fetus . . . it seemed to me then to be very like the polliwogs I hunted in the local streams . . . it was also uniquely animal like. What I learned at my mother's knee was that *we all have evolved* from more primitive forms of life.

Complementing this knowledge was the fact that my two grandmothers loved to discuss our family origins . . . they could trace their family histories to people great and small, dull or interesting, back for many generations in history. And coupled with my mothers' teaching of biological evolution . . . these stories implanted in me the significance of *family origins* . . . of types, nationalities and races. But above all else, I was left puzzling about the oldest human questions: *"From Whence do we come, What are We, and Wither are we Going?"* These same questions have guided my search for the truth in sculpture for my whole life.

These elements within me had to grow through the maturing process before they developed into their final direction. While growing up I attended some 38 different schools. And the circumstance of the economic depression of the 30's gave me a turbulent and varied set of life experiences as I was growing up. Finally at the outbreak of World War II, I joined the Marine Corps and bought the *Notebooks of Leonardo DaVinci* (that guided me into a self-learning process). Later in the war I went to the South Pacific in the Merchant Marine. By the time I finally returned to civilian life I had become a self-directed student of people and the environment. I studied various schools of psychology, philosophy, technology and art and I became an avid museum goer. And as I was studying to becoming a sculptor, I worked at a variety of jobs for several years. During this time, I was set on the course of trying to understand our origins in nature as well as the nature of humanity . . . a course that I continue to this day

*****

I found that in the formation of human character and world view there are two important aspects of experience that determine our evolution . . . these are the **Scope** and **Depth of experience:** Scope relates to the degree of our experience of the earth in terms of weather, season and geographical position on the planet. During my own formative years I lived in a number of places across the North American continent, and later I traveled extensively to Europe, the Middle East and Africa. I, of course, had sailed to the South Seas during World War II, and the sea has always been an important factor in my life. And so I developed a feeling for the planet's variety of place and the variety of its growth (I became an avid landscape watercolorist over the years). I have continued the direct study of nature all my life. Later on I renewed my interest in the movement of water and the currents of the sea, as well as the processes of weather patterns. These more specific studies are related to the **Depth** of my sense of the human figure and its evolutionary origins in the distant past.

Man has always sought varied explanations for our beginnings on the earth. As a child I was told of the biblical explanations for the creation and man's beginning in the fabled Garden of Eden. But during my formative years, in the light of the scientific explanations that were beginning to come forth, I could not accept the biblical attempts to explain the unknown. So I became a Darwinian collector of the factual evidence of our evolution on the planet.

At a crucial point in my development there came to me an additional very important experience that began to assert a great dominance in my understanding of the life process: this was the publication of Wilhelm Reich's book, *Cosmic Superimposition,* that had to do with our own contact with the energy processes of space. Through my studies of this energy, I soon found that all life is imbued with the energy that has formed our galaxy and planetary system. This same energy in its varied phases has formed all of the entities and processes that we know as life. I have written a book for artists called *Abstraction in Art and Nature* that outlines many of the energy processes that can be seen by anyone with the naked eye. This book, I am delighted to say, has been in print for many years. And it is the foundation of the learning processes I have followed in creating the sculptures of the human figure that are shown in this book.

# Images and Commentary

# 1. Old Adam . . . Young Eve

This small bronze bas-relief is the seminal beginning of my approach to the human figure in art. Though I had painted figures and done a number of figure sculptures before I did this work, this piece marked the beginning of my true examination of human expression. There are several reasons for this: one has to do with my rejection of the Biblical version of creation. As charming as the old myth might be . . . it cannot possibly have happened in that fashion . . . when seen in the light of what we now know of evolution. After finishing this work it also marks the point when I started to use the welding process in my sculpture. I had been studying the welding process and metal techniques for several years before this time.

As I had been puzzling about our human origins for some time, I asked myself, how should we look at our ancient ancestors . . . since we can now trace them back to the Olduvai Gorge in Africa some 150,000 years ago? How did these people live; how did they organize their groups; what were their concerns and how did they feel about each other and about their existence?

We modern people have the general misconception that our primitive ancestors were gross, stupid and violent. Actually this is not the case: this is actually a mental projection of emotionally armored and insensitive men . . . men who came into being through the misguided and harmful social practices that occurred at a much later date.

My answer to this ignorance came out of my spirit and my modeling hands and took the form of that hearty, bearded old man who showed his protection to his wife, his daughter or his friend as they sat near their cave in the springtime sun those many years ago. I could never deny this vigorous old spirit . . . as he sat there in his unclothed and strongly sexual body. When this image was complete this question arose in my mind . . . *How did this old fellow feel about himself and about these women?* He sat there with this girl-woman beneath the tree of life (as all trees are Trees of Life) and his vast feelings of love went out from him and his arm circled the shoulder of this female member of his tribe. He protected her, he comforted her and he surrounded her with his love . . . for he was fiercely and deeply honest . . . a true man.

# 2. An Older Eve

This head of Eve has been in my studio for many years. It was completed only a few months after the Old Adam. Originally it was a full-scale head of a woman done in hollow welded steel, however after a couple of year's time I cut the head down to the face we see here. Something about this woman's expression has always haunted me. I never exhibited it; it remained in my studio as a spirit that has lived in my subconscious mind. Only recently have I mounted it on the base shown here and its meaning has become clear to me.

Early in my career I painted many portraits . . . I was very interested in the development of character in both males and females. I felt that the processes of formation of character in portraiture gave the clues to the soul of the person. Yet when I looked at this head of Eve as I had finally made it I was able to look through the eyes to the deeper origins of expression. And I eventually realized that the facial expressions of portraits actually were indications of the deeper realm of feeling and emotion that emerged from the entire body, and it came clear to me that facial expressions are only the surface expressions of any subject's body.

In the intervening years, experience has shown me that there are vast realms of feeling within all parts of the body. There are eloquent and vast meanings stored in the muscles, tendons and fascia of the entire body. Unfortunately they are largely suppressed so that what you see on the portrait face is an amalgam of blocked expressions that are impossible to fathom in the real sense of character understanding.

So this head of Eve has become a symbol of her womanly yearning across the millennial ages. It represents to me the essence of female sorrow. So I have included in the next few pages several more of the modeled heads that I have done over the years to illustrate this point of view.

# 3. A Troubled Man

This head of a middle aged man expresses a restrained and troubled soul. Though on the surface he appears to be a man of confidence and strength, nonetheless his expression of emotion is held within him. Though there seems to be a kindness and the capacity to love that mark his brow and cheeks . . . the emotions held within him are far more powerful and painful than those he is willing to express. It is as though his emotions are warring within his body. His face seems to be in a conflicted state of frozen movement. The emotions warring within him are not resolved . . . so his expression is conflicted.

This sadness and puzzled facial inertia are common to many men in the modern world. It is as though a large part of their histories have been frozen on their faces. I have found that one cannot find the causes of their condition in their facial expressions. They can only be found by looking deeper into the entire body structure.

# 4. A Remorseful Man

This head of a man experiencing remorse seems to be more expressive than the previous portrait, yet it does not tell the entire story of his state of being. His troubled brow points deeper into his emotions and also seems to point downward beyond his head to the mid-region of his body. One feels the need to view his entire figure in order to understand the full sense of his pain. There is also the suggestion that there is another being that is either sharing or causing his hurt.

We become aware that portraits do not usually tell the whole story, but rather suggest that there is far more to be told, the head itself, in its contracted state, tells of a human drama that we need to know more of. Unanswered questions arise: is this man's state of contrition in any way justified . . . or is it an indication of his guilt? Has he committed some crime . . . or is he a man who has been sinned against? Clearly we need to know more of this drama that only full figures can tell.

# 5. Head of a Grieving Man

This portrait head expresses an immense feeling of sorrow and care. The entire head is weighted with grief. This burden of emotion is in no way transient, but it instead shows the great burden of years of oppression. In the brow there is shown the struggle of an extremely kind soul that has carried these unanswered emotions for many years. There is an overwhelming kindness expressed in the cast of the head on the shoulders and body. It is as though the arms have grown weary of reaching out to lost loved ones. This is a noble soul . . . a wonderful human being.

One feels the need to comfort and help this man sustain his hope . . . for he is not alone, but is a man responsible for others who may not understand his warmth of being. So much more could be told by this man's entire figure. This head, as do the others, begs us to know more . . . for the most haunting thing about all three of these portraits is the suggestion that within them there are memories of vast levels of experience and need. A man's capacity to generate life is the largest aspect of his being and it relates to the streams of creative energy that form the galaxy and motivate the planet itself. Manhood is a thing to be worthy of.

# 6. A Sharp-Souled Woman

Unlike the portraits of the males, this woman expresses a powerfully mis-guided sense of her own self-worth, with a sense of self-righteousness that is driven by an overpowering inner determination. On the surface this expression seems to be invincible, yet it is motivated by her even deeper sense of worthless-ness. The expression is of a person driven by an inner need to justify herself by the force of her opinions and her cutting criticism of others. These expressions of inner conflict produce a façade of superiority and disdain that is intended to wither all those who oppose her opinions and attitudes.

What she is actually denying is her own inner feminine nature, a nature that might soothe and comfort those who may need her. This is the strongest female conflict of instincts, and it can produce grief in those around her. This is the most tragic conflict of feminine life as it creates disappointment in all those who come in contact with her. This might never have happened if her true nature had been affirmed in early life.

# 7. Maternal Sorrow

When we look at a portrait of a woman we see not only an individual, but we see the miracle of life before us . . . for women are the bearers of the life force. As a consequence of this, they are the principal guardians of the human emotional life process. They embody *Motherhood* in their entire nature. In the formal aspects of woman there is reproduced the Earth itself . . . she conceives, nourishes and guards the growth of life on a scale that is difficult to conceptualize. A woman is a creature of tremendous power and her body is the emblem of creation. There is tremendous force in womanhood.

Consequently woman is capable of powerful emotions that sweep her soul like the force of an ocean's tide. The sorrow that this portrait head of a woman expresses has the sweep of the ages. And it consumes her entire body . . . her hair, her face and her neck seem to respond to the tide of her body's grief. Perhaps this grief is the result of the death of her child . . . or perhaps it is the loss of a family member or a mate. Whatever it might be these are the emotions that exalt the human race.

# 8. A Woman's Dreams

Because of the powerful nature of a woman's emotions, her capacity to project her feelings in dreams is great. This woman's gentle dreams reflect her capacity to recreate the world. In her sweetest visions she inhabits her dream world with sweet and kindly spirits. Her dreams are visions of what might be when the world is bathed in the light of peace. There is music in her being that floats across the night air and surrounds those she nurtures and loves. She herself is love.

She is a teacher of life . . . and how it might be lived when peace reigns. She is a gardener of the earth . . . planting and arranging the essences of healthy life. She is also the caretaker of birds and pets and the creatures of the land. Her nature is mysterious to man . . . and it will always be so. For she is the dream we follow.

# 9. What are we . . .
# Who are we . . . Why are we?

I made this sculpture realizing that it is only when we look at an overall organization of human families that we can begin to understand the roots of evolutionary and expressive meaning. The sculpture was exhibited in New York at a show of figurative artists organized by the painter John Koch (1909–1979) at an uptown gallery in the early 60's. The exhibition was intended to stimulate an interest in a revival of the figure. It failed in this purpose and Abstract Art continued to dominate the art scene. But it *did* serve a purpose for me as I was able to probe further into the biological and emotional meanings of human form. To understand humanity I saw that one must look at the growth and organization of family groups.

This sculpture served that purpose for me as it fixed the emotional interrelations of male and female parents and children on the earth. But it did not quite answer the questions of form that began streaming in my consciousness. It did however suggest my next more involved composition . . . a composition that called into play some things I had been learning in philosophy and psychology for several years.

# 10. The Ages of Man (perplexed?)

The Ages of Man is a complex composition of 48 human figures representing all the ages of the male and female subjects. It cannot quite be broken down into specific units of composition, but is rather a flow of the various events and relationships that occur as people grow and age in the life process. I composed the piece by depicting an aged man dying and being attended by his wife. This occurs at the end of the stream of figures and is interwoven with two children who pass onward. The composition then moves forward through the grieving relatives to a conflicted family with a pregnant daughter and her young man. The figures continue to stride forward showing family relationships, various friendships, the observers of the distant future, the teaching of children, love relationships . . . and finally at the front of the composition there is a pregnant woman and three boys running into the future. But the exact nature of the relationships is better understood by examining the print of the sculpture itself.

What I concluded from this composition was that the most meaningful relationships of life are those that occur between man and woman . . . that the core of life stems primarily from the embrace of love between man and woman. All else stems from this powerful function of the life process . . . I therefore determined to examine all of life's relationships from the viewpoint of the embrace of life.

# 11. The Beelzebubians (Critics, Experts, Confabulators and Pornographers)

The problem that next arose to me was the question of why has such an open approach to understanding the imagery of the human figure been so completely obscured . . . when it seems so clearly obvious. The answer to this has to do with what I have called *The Beelzebubain Factor* . . . and this relates directly to the problem of sexuality. There has been confusion throughout history of the facts of the biological, emotional, and educational understanding of this all important human function.

Sexuality is the most powerful factor in human emotional life . . . and it is also the most misunderstood, most misused, most exploited and the most feared biological process of them all. The consequences of the misuse of this function are life-shattering to the very core function of human existence. The question of what has caused this turmoil in the practice and understanding of this most vital function becomes the most significant issue to understanding the human imagery process. Jesus said that *The Temple of God is within us* . . . and the ills of the human race can also be traced to our human mental structure. I have termed this disease *Beelzebubianism* after the early name for the devil. And since all devils reside within us . . . we must look to our own capacity to distort human nature to find the source of this evil. Humans are the cause of Human troubles.

In this sculpture I have defined several of the evils of man in humorous and graphic terms. The ranting political Public Relations distorter of history is at the fore front of the tribe and his sycophantic pet dog-man is by his side. The pair of social critics of style and behavior stands behind them. And the applauding matron-patron of the arts stands next to them. While on the right, the philanthropic money man and his haughty companion fill out the gathering of opinion makers. These are the image distorters . . . and their range of power is immense.

# 12. Sacred and Profane Love (The Side-show of Morals)

If we seek to find the causes of the distortion of the male psyche we can find much of it in the fashion in which the female body is projected on the stage of life. Here two young boys watch the side-show of beauty as it is represented in our society. At one side of the stage they see the demure maiden who covers her breast and pudenda in what is actually a provocative manner that seems to say "Look, but don't see." On the other side of the stage is a bawdy hip-slung woman who seems to say, "Look all you want to, for I don't really value any part of my body at all."

The two boys are naturally attracted to the woman who openly displays it all, and this affects their growing consciousness of what seems to be the nature of love. They are not aware *that their own sense of life is being manipulated* . . . and that what they are seeing will remain with them for the rest of their lives . . . unless something unusual occurs to change their vision.

# 13. Spiritual Agony

I have studied human anatomy intensely, and have dissected the human body in medical school. I have, in addition, studied the origins of artistic anatomy in Greek and Roman sculpture . . . and have written about its development in sculpture and painting throughout art history. Art is currently at a point where the understanding of the human figure has met a stone wall, hence the stalemate of figurative art at this time. We have come to a point where the underlying reality of the figure seems beyond comprehension. Tragically, this also reflects the stalemate of our human society that has progressed to the ultimate development of mechanical skills . . . while leaving people in a lonely and helpless state of spiritual ignorance.

This figure expresses this spiritual agony, but it also shows the possible solution to this state of grief. The human body is not just a sum of anatomical parts, but it is primarily a creation of the cosmic substance of life. The figure pulsates with *energy!* It is modeled and formed by this energy . . . the same energy that forms the planet and the galaxies.

This figure has been modeled in living bronze using the oxy-acetylene process. I did this in the awareness of the biological energy processes. I was aware of the ways that *blocked energy* creates misery in human beings . . . and I have shown the despair that this figure experiences through his own state of blocked body energy. So, what follows will be sculptures that have been done with a newer understanding of the figures and their energetic relationship to one another, to the earth and to the galaxy through which the earth travels.

# 14. The Joy of Man and Woman

When the image of love is balanced in the exchange of energy, the thrilling and exalting flow lifts the spirits of the paired lovers beyond the strictures of gravity. Trust, coupled with an atmospheric sweetness, is one of the dominant feelings that ensue. These figures embody the dreams of youth that have enabled the history of life to unfold.

# 15. Man's Dreams of Life

Strength comes to men who see the future expressed in their ability to support the dreams of the women in their life. The energy courses through the man's body and his sense of power infuses his sense of the future. The man's body becomes like the very stream of comic energy as this dream of life fills his soul.

# 16. The Portal of Life

In order for a youth to enter manhood he must enter through the portal of life and choose his mate according to her energetic nature. It is vital that he select a woman with whom his energy intertwines in the enchanting ways of the mystery of life. There is never a set pattern because the pattern occurs when the energy forces of each create a unity that leads them both. Mating is always a mysterious process, because it involves the revelation of opening into a new level of existence for them both. As the relationship proceeds, unknown vistas of the future begin to unfold. And these new vitas challenge both of them to enter the world of the mature future.

# 17. The Vision of Creation (Man's Dreams)

Within each man there dwells the dream of his potential. The dream extends even into future times. The dream is the substance of the creation that fills that passage within his spine that flows from his sacrum, up his spinal column to his ever seething brain. The dream nourishes him and comforts him for it is the eternal gift of his mother who was open to the embrace of the galaxy at the time of his beginning.

Man has been guided by this dream since his first dawn . . . and even before when he was evolving from the lowliest vertebrates. He has reached up in yearning to the heavens from the beginning of time . . . searching to be worthy of life.

# 18. The Family

Man and Woman are a unity that comes together to create the actual purpose of their lives . . . the family organism. But the growth of human intelligence has brought added difficulties to the evolutionary progress of these family organisms. As the physical problems of existence have been solved . . . food supply, housing, transportation, education and economics . . . the ability of the human mind to understand and cope with this progress has been overwhelmed by a flood of new images and new choices. This deluge of product and imagery has created a confused, puzzled and emotionally over-charged people who cannot find their way in the stream of life.

The family of today has lost its basic unity . . . its basic contact with its energetic roots in the cosmos. The natural energetic roles of mother, father and children have become blurred and the *seeking* nature of the family organism has lost its meaning. Yet it struggles onward in search of the goal of life.

# 19. The Family Search for Wisdom

In order to perpetuate itself the family organism must search for the planetary and galactic wisdom to continue life. First the man and woman must find accord in their deepest energetic souls to find that pathway to a harmonious future place of existence, a place where they can grow and prosper . . . each in their own way. They look to the seasons of the planet, to the processes of the life forms around them. They look to the progress of the planets passage through the stars in the heavens. And from all of these things truths are revealed to them.

# 20. The Greatest Truth (Above all things . . . protect the young)

The greatest truth of all is to nurture and protect the young. For children, in their learning, must wander and ramble, and taste whatever is at hand, whatever seems to attract . . . until their senses are developed and they have grown their capacities to protect themselves. To learn to know how far one can go from home, and to know the difference between what is good and what is harmful. And then to gain the ability to discriminate between images of good and evil, as well as between persons of good and evil. And later, to see beyond the horizon . . . to other people and other lands. That is the purpose of life.

# 21. The Path Revealed . . .
## is the Heavenly Energy

When humanity has learned to live the truth by respecting the energy within themselves and the blossoming energy within their newborn children . . . the path will be revealed to them. They will then begin to form a civilization that honors all of life's creation and they will tend the garden of the planet earth into a limitless future.

# 22. The Energy of the Galaxy Swings Through Life

The surge of joyous recognition of galactic energy fills humankind with unbounded enthusiasm for the heaven's glory. And so we reach out toward the cosmic streaming with a sense of the awesome creation of all life. Filled with religious fervor we cry out, ***"This is the God we have sought since our beginning on the earth!"***

All of the religions of the earth were founded by people who have sensed the infinite Glory of Creation. All religions have come about as the result seeking for the ultimate truth. We must recognize ***this truth*** of the harmony man ***can*** possess . . . when this is finally understood humankind will know peace.

# 23. The Human Family Circle

Strength comes to the man who can recognize and give in to the creative process of the energy field within himself. Such a man is endowed with the strength and ingenuity to support his mate in her goal to create a family organism. Their children complete the divine circle that rotates in its own unique way of individuality . . . never creating people that are quite the same as others, but always keeping within the laws of life.

# 24. The Wheel of Life

The Wheel of Life is an ancient Buddhist symbol of the continuity of the life process through time. This symbol is an apt representation of how the life of man is maintained by the lawfulness of the cosmic energy processes. It very beautifully reproduces the superimposition of the galactic energy streams that were described by Wilhelm Reich in his *Cosmic Superimposition.* The Wheel of Life also reproduces our planet's formation and its progress through the solar system. In other words it symbolizes the *lawfulness* of the life process.

Our laws were given to us by the man *Moses* who was said to have been given them by God himself on Mount Sinai. I too have climbed this mountain, although I did not see a personified God, I still somehow feel that these ten laws were truly *the Laws of Life.* For they keep humankind on the pathway of the Galactic Energy Process. Therefore, I submit my Wheel of Life to you for your consideration.

# 25. The Compassionate Love of Life

One of the strongest tenets of many of our religions, be they Christian, Hebrew, Buddhist or others, is that compassionate treatment of the injured, the sick and the fallen is most proper. It is generally agreed that this is the way that society should react. This lawful recognition stems from our love of the life within us, and also from the belief that it is derived from *God.* In our time we may infer that the name of **the most holy** is also the name of the *Creative Energy of the Universe.* This has always seemed most reasonable to me . . . as it more accurately describes the author of our being.

Though this form of composition is usually said to depict the Deposition of Jesus from the Cross, to me it is more a symbol of the origin of all *Healers* . . . persons who by their touch can heal the soul as well as the body.

# 26. The Healer

Though I was raised by people who espoused their faith in the biblical and divine man called Jesus, I do not today believe in his divinity. Instead, I see him as one of the greatest healers who ever lived. I have given the religion of the Christian Church much thought. I later made a trip to the Holy Land, where I came to see Jesus as a man who had an instinctive insight into the energy processes that moved in people. His wonderful words, *"The temple of God is within you,"* have been the guiding message of my life since that time. I cannot believe in the old mystical explanations of the origins of life either . . . for we know far deeper truths today.

I think of my early days in the orphanage in 1932 when I was seven, and remember that the orphanage was just a few blocks north of Cal Tech, where the astronomer Edwin Hubble was working at the telescope at Mount Wilson Observatory mapping the galaxies and discovering that our planet existed in a cosmos of millions of galaxies. I remember too, the kindly minister who visited the boys in the house where I lived and who taught me the 121$^{st}$ Psalm that went *"I will lift up mine eyes unto the hills from whence cometh my help"*. And I saw those hills as Mount Wilson . . . even in those days.

So my image of Jesus the healer has come to be one of a man who loved children . . . and who saw deeply into the heart of humankind. For many years I wondered how I might represent him in sculpture. There are so many examples that show that suffering, crucified soul. But my image has turned out to be quite different: it is drawn from the words of a Roman writer who scoffed at the figure of Jesus as being *"Only fit for slaves, women and children."* To my way of thinking this version describes the true man. I hope you will find meaning and comfort in this work. By his loving touch he could move the energy in all his patients.

# 27. The River of Life Flows Onward (an after image of the Ages of Man)

Although the fate of the human race is in the hands of each of us . . . for we all bear the stream of life within us . . . we each must determine what we can do to perpetuate the flow of energy in all living things. Our principal task is to insure that our children maintain the unimpeded flow of energy in their bodies. Although it is certain that all children will suffer some emotional and physical shocks that cause the flow of energy to be at times slowed down . . . we must guard against any permanent armoring of the body's emotions and mobility. To do this we must first make the effort to learn the human anatomy growth process and structure from the embryo to adulthood. Once this is learned it is essential to understand how the body's energy processes relate to the various emotional expressions and release.

The human body is itself constructed of emotional processes that are engendered by the flow of energy within the several systems that make up the physical structure. Each of these systems pulse with specific rhythms: the Lymph, the Veinous Fluid and the Cerebrospinal Fluid . . . all of which flow in specific ways in the body and relate to the emotional balance of the whole being. It might even be said that once the embryo leaves the fluid of the mother's amniotic shelter . . . the life in the child flows onward in the individual. It is my understanding that the energy of the galaxy pulses in a variety of ways in all of these fluids that make up the individual person.

As a sculptor of the human figure I feel that awareness of these pulsations of life are as important for the artist to project as are the patterns of the bone and muscular structure that enfold them. If they are absent from the artist's perception his work remains merely a mechanical representation that is devoid of true life. The danger in figurative art is that some artists become very adept at producing these show pieces of false life. And they erect their tableaus of fraudulent personalities and histories in public squares across the world. These are the skilled mechanics of the art world, and they know not what they do. But a little more concentration on studying the life within themselves and time to reflect will no doubt clear the air of their souls—and give the world much better images.

Strength comes to the man who can recognize and give in to the creative process of the energy field within himself. Such a man is endowed with the strength and ingenuity to support his mate in her goal to create a family organism. Their children complete the divine circle which rotates in its own unique way of individuality, never creating people that are quite the same as others, but always keeping within the laws of life.

# BOOKS BY NATHAN CABOT HALE

*Creating Welded Sculpture*
Watson-Guptil, New York, 1968
Dover Press Edition with new foreword and final chapter, 1994

*The Embrace of Life (the sculpture of Gustav Vigeland)*
Abrams, New York, 1969

*Abstraction in Art and Nature*
Watson-Guptil, New York, 1972
Dover Press Edition with new introduction, 1993

*The Birth of a Family (a book on natural childbirth)*
Anchor Press, New York 1979

*The Spirit of Man*
Dyer (medical arts), 1981

*Fox Tails* (a book of poems)
White Whale Press, Amenia, New York, 1993

*The Elephant's Peaceable Kingdom* (a book of Fables)
White Whale Press, Amenia, New York, 1999

*On The Perception Of Human Form In Sculpture*
White Whale Press, Amenia, New York, 2000

*The Van Zanzibar Testaments* (a parody of mystical religion)
White Whale Press, Amenia, New York, 2004

*Finding the Human Image*
*In Life, Sculpture and Painting*
White Whale Press, Amenia, New York, 2005

*Exploring The Roots Of Human Expression In Sculpture*
White Whale Press, Amenia, New York, 2007

White Whale Press
57 Sheffield Road
Amenia, New York 12501
845 373 9380
www.agesofman.org

Nathan Cabot Hale's working years
# CHRONOLOGY

| | |
|---|---|
| 1961 | *On The Removal of Fig Leaves* (brochure on the Figure) |
| 1962 | Magnetic Field Studies |
| 1968 | Developed Ages of Man concepts 1969 |
| 1968 | Traveled to Spain and Portugal |
| 1968 | *Creating Welded Sculpture* Published |
| 1969 | Traveled to Greece |
| 1969 | Biographical research on Wilhelm Reich in Europe and Washington, DC |
| 1970 | Ages of Man Foundation begun |
| 1970 | Purchased White Whale building in Amenia |
| 1972 | *Abstraction in Art and Nature* published |
| 1972–74 | Published article "Galactic Superimposition," Part I and II |
| 1973 | Made pilgrimage to the Holy Land |
| 1974 | Bachelor of Science in The Morphology of Form in Art |
| 1975 | *The Function of Sequestration in Galactic Energy Fields* |
| 1976 | PhD in Morphology |
| 1976 | Gave Independent Lecture Series on Art History |
| 1976–75 | NYU Lecture Series on Morphology in Art |
| 1977 | European researches of Round Churches |
| 1978 | Malta researches for the *Birth of a Family* |
| 1979 | *Birth of a Family* published |
| 1981 | *The Spirit of Man* published |
| 1982 | Ireland lectures on art |
| 1985–88 | Senior Editor of *Art/World* |
| 1988 | Member of Century Association |
| 1989–92 | Wrote a series of 300 poems |
| 1990 | Did *Christ Sculpture* (an important experience) |
| 1993 | *Fox Tails* published |
| 1995 | Briefly editor of *Sculpture Review* |
| 1999 | *Elephant's Peaceable Kingdom* published |
| 2000 | *On the Perception of Form in Sculpture* published |
| 2002 | Wrote "The Orphanage" published in *Journal of Orgonomy* |
| 2004 | *The Van Zanzibar Testaments* published |
| 2005 | *Finding the Human Image* published |
| 2007 | *Exploring the Roots of Human Expression in Sculpture* published |